for the ghosts we cannot keep in the grave
and the poetry that comes from their haunting.
i do not regret loving you. i regret not being
able to understand your definition of what
love meant for you. i regret spending all
those years fighting for someone who gave
up on me when they had a plan all along
to never see us through.

-karnes-

When Goodbye Becomes You Vol.2

In Bed. In Life

5am finds me more often here. an early morning is the most serene feeling that exists for me. before most awake, i've already lived a few dreams. coffee tastes the best just before dawn. the aroma sings out a song i go to bed ready to hear. being the only one up, sitting with silence and your thoughts, the world seems to pause for you. the birds rest in a breeze. the wind itself stops howling long enough to recognize a submitted silence. your body wakes up slowly, then all at once, as you have your first sip. i write down a few things in my journal before any light appears through the window to read what i have written down. writing in darkness has its advantages, because we are all someone else in this quiet hour before remembrance finds us. before memories call out for your attention. i check on you to make sure you are still sleeping, to make sure you are taken care of and in a gentle state of breathing. i close the door quietly, then make another cup of coffee to ensure i am fully awake by the time the stars fade away. i hear you get up or at least trying to get out of bed. i know you love your rest. i haven't figured out how you like your coffee in the morning, so i wait and watch you make it, waiting for you to join me on the couch. your morning kisses are just as strong and needed as any coffee that has tried to waken and enliven what still remains stagnant in me. i hold you and feel a warmth of a thousand suns. a thousand fires looking for more earth to burn. innocence finds us right before we begin making plans for our day. i listen to you intently, hoping i don't miss a single thing you need to tell me. there's something to be said about communicating openly, without passing over or glancing through what is actually being said. acknowledgement comes in all forms, but when i go to hold you, i know what it means to me. i know how long it's been since anyone held me with the same love in return. each morning has been this way with you. me being unable to sleep longer has nothing to do with you being here. my body is trying to catch up to this dream, this life, the anticipation of early morning coffee with you. i know everything i feel today, will be felt again tomorrow and however many cups we share together. what a life it would have been if i could have given you what you needed. now, i am drinking this coffee alone, looking at where we once sat and talked about growing old together.

A World Full Of Sadness And Hopeful Hoping

if you come back to me eighty and gray, i will love you with however many years i have left to give you before the grave takes the rest. i've had ten people tell me they wanted to divorce their significant other. i've had eight people tell me they lost a loved one. i've had five people tell me they have cancer. i've had four people tell me they almost overdosed. i've had three people tell me they wanted to kill themselves. i've had two people tell me they were in love, but afraid to say anything. i've had one person tell me how much medicine they take to function properly. there is only one of me, but some days, one is enough. we are all going through something horrible, but hopefully good, too. this job takes a lot out of me, and i can only hope i have some left at the end of the day to give back to you what you give to me.

When The Pain Stops

my clarity is found daily by the stories i hear but never talk about. i won't list everything i have heard within the last week alone. i write to say this, i am sorry for what you are going through. i still have my bad days. i still have far more good ones though now that i express myself through writings. it doesn't fix a life. it can only make you see more of it in a more coherent way. most of the messages i get are someone dealing with their own trauma and loss. they tell me, thank you. i reply back, thank you for fighting with a bravery not everyone can see. words alone cannot heal what hurts, but they can stop it long enough to know one day it will.

Groundhog Day Again

i haven't had peace in months, maybe since i was born barely breathing. i am content being alone, but this missing grows old the older i get and the further away i find myself, from myself. if telling you, i love you, doesn't mean anything anymore, i will practice telling it to myself and see how that feels for a change. i wake up missing you, like i did yesterday, like i did today. life is all the same when you are constantly trying to find what you have lost.

The Flower And Its Song Of Mercy

i find you to be the most intriguing and intrinsic soul i have come across during my visit here. life won't always go your way nor will it be fair, but you have given me a second chance to believe in everything good again. of all the flowers i have planted for you along the way, the sun remains in your favor. you give the birds their morning song, their astute awakening. there is a promise they hold tight within their tiny bellies. one made of commitment and sacrifice to insure the dawn knows it won't ever open its eyes and be alone without their reassuring sound of light and love.

A Grace Named Infinity

she's the golden hour, made from a million suns and a single moon. a beauty to be felt, to be seen, to be handled with a love as gentle as waves breaking over a true dawning. a fighter down to her bones, being broken raised her to survive a winter's cold while being okay with how alone this place makes you feel. when it comes to love, a heart must become ardent if living is what you are after. be gentle, dear child. be brave, sweet evergreen. breathing in chaos does not make you become it. it is all in the wind. it is in all of the places you feel most alive. lonely is not your name. you are infinite, as is your grace, as is the way you complete the sky by becoming the shine and shimmer.

<u>As Doubt Becomes A Slow Death</u>

i lean into this feeling, this tangible sensation of longing for closeness. i am running out of ways to hide your name, but i won't surrender it while i still have breathing left to do. i could have loved you until we both became faceless. at night when it is just me and my thoughts, i play back all the times i held you and i am forced to live in the now without you. there is not a more unbearable thought than believing you are there possibly thinking of me, but you cave into your stubbornness, as i reach back into mine. sitting here, i am sure i forgot how i never held you more than a few times, but it will always feel like a lifetime i had with you.

<u>The Reflection We Cannot Embrace</u>

my mind is a precarious place. a misleading step into a grace without safety to take me away. my scars are no longer my enemy. now, they are the only friends around me. i look at my life and wonder when it got so empty. i look at old pictures and realize we are all just humans in other people's memories. darkness creeps in, and the light teaches it how to shine, instead of reflecting death from inside of my own eyes.

A Blinding Force Called Forgiveness

love is a misconception led by those confused with a defined dictation and enunciation for things not working out in their favor. love is tasteless, shapeless, blind, and limbless, but it always finds its way to those who love it as if it were everything, because those who have something to believe in, have never been without it. each time these lungs think of giving in and giving up, i feel the pull from the stars to not only live more, but remember why i am still here in the first place and what my meaning is to those around me and to myself. it is a powerful realization once you understand how many times you should have died, but you made it out still standing whole and completed, while so many you have known and loved are no longer here by your side. do not take this fucking gift for granted. i beg you.

A Wandering Heart

there's a great sense of wander in the hearts of those who stay wild for the universe. they are the ones who drink straight from the cosmos each night. i have spent years admiring you from afar as you are. you are more than just a woman drifting. you are a soul of light, a genuine wonderment of bones and sunflowers. many anticipate to be that way, to be outlined by transparency. no one else will ever be the truest show of reflection for beauty and roses. maybe one day i can have the opportunity to find you again, just as the sun does with the moon.

Red Rover

red rover, red roses, come over and in from the cold. you are shaking, a body collapsing into itself. it has been days since i have seen you, felt you, heard your name roll out of my mouth. the roof of this place is barely being held together, but we never would have stayed here for long if not for the shelter it gave to us. we didn't need forever. we didn't need tomorrow. humans like us, survivors, make it on nothing by having everything at our fingertips. gardens cry out to you, the gentle guardians of youth and rebel. i forgot what missing something like this felt like. i forgot it breaks you at the bone and tears at your fibers. i forgave the storms and all the tragedies. they did not know by trying to kill me, they restored my love for living once again. a peasant like me could never be a king, but my sword remains sharp with a mighty swing. i will take out all the devils for you to have the angels on your side.

<u>Halfway Here And There</u>

the fear we keep can only hold us hostage if we allow it to grab us by the throat and choke out our truth. i am not human and have difficulty understanding the eyes of those who do not see what i see. i am learning how to feel everything around me without it taking from my own energy. i do not fear the darkness. i do not fear the solitude. i am caught in-between this world and the next, a fish halfway out of the net. when i think about this life, even angels love to burn.

The Entanglement

i want to spend my life making sure you know how it feels to have someone who will always love you for the unexplainable ways you laugh to hide your tears. how you fight back the pain and confront it with your endearing sense of dark humor. how you go to sleep with your socks on, and by the time you wake up, they are missing in another world. how you giggle when there is an awkward silence to make the worst situation feel like the most unforgettable experience. how when you blink, the sun inches towards you to be closer without making it obvious to others. i want to spend my life making sure the inner child in you never dies and celebrating the way we never act our age. we may be reckless. we may be out of control. we may be more than love can keep together, but we were made to be free and youthful together, while reinventing new ways to stay as naked as we can throughout the day. there is nothing that feels as good as your soul does when it is on mine, all entangled and nudging closer for more.

Turn Your Lights On

being here has been my greatest dream. i don't believe in religion, but i do believe in finding yourself. i believe you should be where your soul desires. i believe in freeing your mind and body from anything that does not serve them. i believe happiness can be a creation you make for yourself regardless of what is happening in your life. i still have a lot of life to search through. i still have a million sensations to feel while i am here and lively. i still have unexpected and unforeseen words, emotions, breaths, and living to unearth, to call my own while i am here. i have always been good at being by myself, alone, on my own. allowing myself to be caught up in-between the mountain's company is enough to forget i am alone. there is magic in finding possibilities where you never once saw yourself growing and evolving. there is hope where you once thought you could never go again.

<u>Of All The Battles</u>

there are words we will search for until
our lungs fall from these bodies. when we
find them, they will appear simple,
powerful, and everything we have
needed since our hearts laid beaten
and defeated by the excursion.

Do It For Yourself For Once

you will always be too much for people. you are not here to seek validation from others. you are not here to beg for love. you are not here to sit and waste your time worrying if maybe they are thinking of you as much as you do of them. you are not here to dwell on the bullshit so many of us get caught up in during our days. be better than that. ask more from yourself and make damn sure you are putting and focusing all of your energy on things that fucking matter, not just some idea of what could happen if you did this or that. do something you love and find gratitude for doing it. exceed your own expectations. be your own reason to try more and give up less on your goals. no one is going to fucking hold your hand while you walk to your next destination. shit doesn't work that way once you get older than seven or eight. i didn't have anyone back then to hold my hand. i walked where i wanted to and it wasn't always the right choice, but i still found a way to make it a part of my life and find truth in my decisions. i can be a horrible friend. i can be a calloused human. i can be the worst person you ever want to meet if you push me to that point. once i am there, all feelings and intentions go out of the window. savagery at its finest. i am not proud of it. i am learning how not to be so cold, but there are monsters running around everywhere and it is so easy to be one at times. it is only then that people get the hint to not bring their negative energy and bullshit to my life or place it outside of my door, expecting me to pick it up, shake it, and say, thank you. people will always run back to what's normal and what makes them feel safe even if it is destined to fail as it did before. even when who they loved and would have died for did something incredibly unforgivable to them. sadly, it is life for those who decline the opportunity to change their patterns for themselves. i am looking for survivors. for the ones who never stop running to the next thing. for the ones who just want to be happy and be forgotten by those who find safety in comfort. there aren't many of us left in this world, but hopefully along this path, they will come out of hiding and shine their faces once again. this world needs them. we all need them if we are being honest with ourselves. they bring the colors out of the trees, sky, and all living things.

When There Is No Replacement For Love

some days i have to remember you're gone. i know as long as there is a breath in my body, it will always belong to you. this year has been like the last three that's come and gone. more chaos. more uncertainty. more war. the rich have a funny way of losing money and the poor have a deathbed full of things they will die trying to save. i have never fit into a category nor have i even cared enough to sit where others speak about good times without knowing what one really is. i have a new smile i have barely used and others have rarely seen. it is not because i am unhappy. it is because i am relearning what it means to be in that state of mind. before i met you, i knew how to hide in the largest of rooms with a few humans roaming the hallways, looking for someone to trade their sorrows with. now, i walk around in plain sight without anyone attempting to approach me with their worries, because everyone has more today than they know what to do with. they remain silent on what's hurting, hoping the coping gets easier to deal with over time. i knew from an early age, before the day woke up nestling birds i keep safe behind my eyes, the hardest fight we have is within. not everyone makes it back from heartache, from an unstaged agony where lovers portray a type of violence meant to be played out before meeting. i have seen hatred look a lot like compassion when it comes from suppressing what you do not want to get out. we were born with a forgiveness meant for those who adored us, and yet, we still fall short of being human. highways taught me how much life there is outside of the lines we are told to stay between. unambiguous interpretations and unrequited feelings shaped me before i ever killed in the name of love. we are told to never harm anyone, yet it is all we know how to do once an emptiness becomes a home you are accustomed to living in. as i look outside these windows, i watch another blue sky turn to black. i knew when i met you, i would either spend the rest of my life loving you or missing you. i thought i was prepared for the latter, but if it isn't you, it will be me and the moon you left behind. there is no replacing a best friend you fell in love with, and are still in love with.

When 3AM Becomes Last Call

i have always wanted certain things more than i should. it is being cursed to love too much or to give someone more than they are worthy of having. it is thinking you never have what you need, but knowing somehow you will figure it out because you have already spilled your blood for the moon to see. you have already broken your bones for the earth to feel. you have already made a traveler out of your sorrows. my proverbial enemy has been me and the demons that seem to laugh at the thought of leaving. i have wanted days to end because the night was a better friend when i was lonely. i have wanted love and all of the pain that rolled in drunk at 3am when fighting over wrong and right seemed like a logical excuse not to sleep or a way of showing someone you cared enough to stay awake until it was settled. i have wanted a better childhood for the kids i will never have. the mere thought of them being born and mirroring my life scared the complete shit out of me. certain things i have squandered in the past come back to me when i least expect them to. certain memories flood my blood and leave me stumbling in the hallways of minds i have stayed in. i once thought i was better off alone until you showed me how it feels to have the wind touch your skin with the intention of adoring the cracks it got through to soothe the humanly ache we all live with. i look at you and see someone i could never give enough to and will always want more of when the years change my bodily form. i am certain about the love you have. i am certain you will take care of all the things i feel are wrong with who i am. i am certain i will still look at you when we are in bed and think to myself how one person can change the course of a thousand lives simply by being comfortable knowing there is still love to be made in the rise and fall of women and men. there is still love to be found and gathered in the arms of the hopeless who let go of everything because having anything is too much and not enough at the same time. i am guilty of overdoing everything i have ever thought of or put the sword to. i cannot love enough, just as i cannot water enough those i love, which ends up killing any chance of us making it out together with our heads above the water and lungs full of breathable air.

In Every Life, In Every Sense of Breathing

here's the complete truth, i never thought i'd love again after her. you came along and showed me something different, a kind of preciousness without harm. i won't ever be able to think of love and it not be you. you didn't ruin me. you changed my entire perspective of what we can endure, of what we are worthy of having, even if it doesn't stick around for the ending. if it isn't you, all i will do is ruin anyone who believes they can love me or wants to be with me, not knowing i see you when they see me. it's tragic i guess. it's apropos as well. when we found each other, i finally felt something other than my demons playing with my bones and breaking my dreams over them. it felt as though i was stumbling out of my own darkness, then there you were, holding a smile fit for a victory i had never been a part of. you freed me from completing another disastrous attempt at being human, when i had not been one of those in years. i was too reckless for my own good, drinking away what was left of my youth. i will never completely understand your leaving and why it ended as abruptly as it started, but i know we were not meant for a lifetime. i take you wherever i go. i can only write about you, because it has always been for you. in this distance between hearts, my body embodies a celestial sensation made from galaxies and moons no longer close enough for me to see. the time twists and bends itself around my mind, making me believe you will always love me, but i honestly think you will never stop. maybe that is the hardest part of it all. maybe knowing i will never be able to be with anyone else and not see you is the endless curse i will carry with me until my head falls off. you were worth it then, and you are worth it now. whatever is inside of me, whatever attached itself to you over the years, it won't let you go. i have tried to leave it where you left it, but even on my thousandth attempt, it still clings to you, as the sun embraces a moon it will perpetually burn for. humans come and go in our lives. it has been that way since chaos found us and turned us into whatever this existence is. i can write all i want about it. i can speak until my tongue is bitten off and rolls slowly down the back of my throat. even then, my soul will find a way to yours to tell you, i love you, in this life, too. you told me you never had anyone fight for you, anyone who wanted to help you battle what's been in your life before. you told me the doubts you have and i spoke of the fears i have. we both know the path isn't always golden. sometimes, it is baptized and paved with a certain kind of darkness that scares away anything resembling light. but not this time. my demons won't ever speak your name. they won't ever choke me out of loving you. they won't ever come fucking near you. my struggles aren't yours. my shortcomings aren't yours. i will readily pick up your sword when you are weary and tired. i will hold your half-broken shield when your shrinking arms become water. i am here for you. i will keep coming back to you. i am writing this after a day of you exploring and me sleeping without you again. i hate waking up and not finding your body. it is the cruelest way to breathe if anyone were to ask me, but what is life if not struggling to find something more than what we have been without. i do not always like to sound as if i am writing poetry in my responses to you. they are my truths though. i am missing you more tonight than yesterday. if that continues, i will have to drive up there sooner than i thought. if i can grow old with you in whatever way this path chooses, that is what i want. if i can hold you and forget about the world for a while, that is what i want. i hope to never make you doubt anything i say or do for you. i hope you feel me when you become constantly overwhelmed with fears of not knowing what to do or what comes next with us. i love your heart. i love your soul. i love your mind. everything that is you, i love. i don't need anything else. i want to be home with you near me. i will keep holding you until you become a part of me. not just a single part, but my entire fucking existence, my entire book of words. we will find all the ways there are to have our life together. i promise you. i am going to love you until all that is left are our bones and a story to tell about who we were and how much we loved. that is a fucking promise. i will type it, say it, and scream it at the stars, always, you are mine, you are mine, you are mine. you are my human. i know it. you are the author of my movements. when i woke up to you the first morning, i knew it was the last time i would ever wake up alone. months have passed since i typed this. we no longer share the same heart. we no longer have promises to make because they broke the day we broke each other's heart.

<u>*When Dreams Aren't Enough*</u>

you told me, "i cannot even begin to tell you how many times in the last two years that i have asked myself if it was ever going to be okay again. if i was ever going to be, normal, again. if the heaviness was ever going to lift, because i was too heavy inside for every person i came into contact with. time goes on and you begin to feel lighter little by little. but there has still been a level of depth i had yet to find, until you. i haven't felt like anyone could meet me where i was and hold my heart with care. it is exhausting having to verbalize every single need and expectation to someone who doesn't have ears to hear or eyes to see. i say nothing to you and you hear me. you give me everything i have always needed and never had." i have never met anyone like her. i replied, "we have been on the same path ever since we began working on ourselves." i never thought i would be able to accept anyone again. i never thought i could see myself being with someone again. i literally thought i was broken and cursed forever after what i thought was the last time i had to explain and show who i was to someone i loved. i have never had someone reciprocate back to me what i give. i have never met a heart or soul like mine that could do something even close to resembling such a thing, until you. i knew i was getting closer to it, closer to you. no more exhaustion of worrying if someone would be able to hear me and see me. i cannot wait to see where this goes with you. i cannot wait to wake up to you. it has been over a decade since i have had anyone to wake up to. you forget what living actually is when you are constantly dying for someone you have never met, someone who you hope to be your first for everything. the beginning, middle, and end. that is what i am doing here with you. it is why my relentlessness is yours, forever and without doubt sleeping next to me. we are one day closer to the other. a place i was not sure existed after experiencing all of the tragedies my eyes have had to love to make sense of how it would play a part in my life. i look forward to lying down with you, interlocking our fingers, and sleeping soundly with our breath and dreams in sync. if this is a dream, may our souls be able to live within it, in every way they can, for as long as they can.

<u>*The Flowers I've Planted*</u>

i find you to be the most intriguing and intrinsic soul i have come across during my visit here. life won't always be easy nor will it be fair, but you have given me a second chance to believe in everything good again. of all the flowers i have planted for you along the way, the sun remains in your favor. you give the birds their morning song, their awakening.

<u>*When Want And Need Changes*</u>

maybe i wanted too much when i asked you for a love you told me you could give. laying in beds of flowers and bones, a final resting place of a promise shot down before it could run, before it could even call out, mother. there is no photo of your pretty face i could take that could show just how lucky i was to know a soul like yours. i take a seat and hold my knees to my chest, as i breathe in the finest air under an endless fiery sun. my eyes will scour a million just to remember everything i saw in you. i will blink once more to begin again, to show myself ghosts only haunt us if we die with them. to show myself how to live if we believe the sorrow transforms into a bluer sky.

<u>SOULMATES</u>

stay a little while longer with your head near my collar. i have never felt such a gentleness, a glorified ease of human upon another. as the sun begins its descent down the belly of the sky, my eyes turn towards you, as we both try and compartmentalize where this memory of ours will go. a wish made is heaven sent once you let go of reality and drift off with your lover. i will never ask or want you to keep me safe. i am going to linger here with you until the bones of my body become another story told about finding a soulmate and how they die together, when growing old was never an ending meant for this world to relish.

Divorcing Thoughts

you are getting married soon and i am still married to the thought of you, to who we were before the ring was given to you by someone you told me you'd never go back to. so i will sit at the graveside and wait for more flowers to accompany me, while you throw your bouquet into a crowd dying to be engaged. i thought if i kept showing you how much i needed you, you would tell me the same. unrequited love is something i was not born with or born to give. eight years ago this november, i finally learned your name. eight years this november, it will all change again. we shared an angel number, and it just so happens to be when you will wed. if that isn't a crushing defeat, losing you all over again surely is. i am happy for you. this is where i leave you for good. after all, happy endings only go to the princess who chooses her prince after midnight strikes and leaves everyone else not good enough for love at first-sight.

When Light Changes

you tried loving the darkness out of me.
i never had someone go beyond what i gave.
you showed me not all light is meant to kill
you where you stand. you showed me how
hands can become a forest of gentleness
where peace takes the place of a ravaged
mind. you once created art to show me who
you were. i shared these writings with you to
allow you closer into my world. i never tried
to scare you away, which was the first time
i had not done it. i should've known then my
monsters and the ones you carried would
have been able to become less of who we
were and more of a passing thought meant
to only scare away those who never knew
what common ground was.

A Beggar's Son

what am i supposed to do with all this missing, when my lips beg of sunlight and love when you are gone? tell me where to rest this weary, this absence of my own heart and mind. for now, i will give it to this rage, this broken state of living i find myself a part of while we remain apart from the line we drew in the earth that represented a distance we would never succumb to. i went from having you curled into me, watching tv, having my eyes on you, locking the front door, then laying down next to you, to reminding myself life doesn't work out the way we think when love becomes something all strangers have in common who swore they knew they would make it. you and i were never made for simply a passing glance. you are still the body i want beside me while breathing, and in the end when death is nothing more than a new beginning to love beyond what was in us to give.

All Relative

pain is my brother, and we have been going at it for years. i wish i knew how to be better at loving things that didn't love me in return. maybe it was a mistake believing in angels appearing for the pure sake of saving face. it infuriates me how i have wanted you more ever since that day you told me you needed my safety. i wish i knew why my mind overthinks everything despite my heart breaking each time i see someone with your face. i am an oak split in two, with roots fighting frost and freeze to make it through another winter without being cut down for firewood. the good in me left the day i attended my first funeral. i learned then how quickly the dead teach us what to love and what we should forget.

When Poetry Proposes

love, sit with me, show me how to correct my posture, and how to hold these eyes from falling back behind me when life doesn't see what i do. i remember being as young as a blade of grass in the summer time, unsure of my place in this world. i looked to you for guidance, for some form of truth. i am constantly watching the sun rise and fall back down to me without anyone to hear my joy, my smile, my laughter. it is a funny thing how much we keep to ourselves when all we want to do is tell someone about a moment of our day when all we did was think of them until the blue turned to night and the moon brought our souls to life. poetry is more than words for me. it is the only love that has never asked me for anything by to be truthful and bleed openly as it does for me.

War And Dawn

i never had walls until you left. these insides have turned sour and my gardens are without a flower to give to anyone asking more from me. i am tired, starving, and worn out from surviving without the proper tools to feed and shelter me from this bitter cold. the only fire i have to speak of, is this hell you gave to me upon your removal from my life. i will manage and get by, burning one page at a time to keep this flame on my body. if i have to, i will hunt down the wolves to help me with my strides. and when death had its hands around my vocal chords, asking me to call out to someone else, i still fucking screamed out your bloody name in hopes of a release. i still fucking fought while you were running away. as the infant snow falls, i will remember you as you were, smaller than all the mighty giants, but still as graceful as birds readying for war and dawn.

The Trees We Become

when this earth finally gets to embrace you, as your last breath becomes every word i write, i will visit you often and tell you how beautiful you have made the flowers, the trees, and every living thing that gets to love you as much as this soul in me. i will come to you every chance i get to tell you the words i wrote for you, but never sent. when i told you there was no one else for me but you, you laughed as if it wasn't true. until my timber body gets to lay somewhere beside you, just know part of me is already in the ground, not knowing what missing you will ever feel like.

The Halves We Need

she was always wanting to believe in something more, something that could take away the pain without losing herself to find it. love was always a prayer, a softly spoken truth she felt deep within her struggle for living a full life. she was a bit manic and chaotic, but she knew it would take losing her mind to find something that would stay. love may be a lot of things for others, but for her, it represented becoming more of herself and learning how to fly with broken wings. trusting yourself through healing is all we can hope for when we are searching for something greater to aspire to be, to give life to, and eventually become. may love never pause before it holds you. may it always be an extra heart when your own breaks in two.

<u>Jubilancy</u>

there will be days that test you even after the confession of a moon placed in the darkest of skies. the eyes of beauty don't always see what is inside that makes it shine after the night calls on the stars to fall. i know this phase may feel helpless to you. i know the emptiness precedes the truth of how it became real in the first place. an angel's face won't always reflect happiness and light. sometimes, it reflects a pain not many will ever know about. wings carry more than the breeze. they're an institution of awareness for what's below them. may you know what it feels like to lay down and not feel a world's worth of weight sitting on top of you. keep your energy close and surrounded by a love only you can give. giving a breath meaning is what love is about. may your lungs open again to a newness, to a radical transformation of soul and bone. grow with the life around you, just as the flower penetrating its own doubt. may you never break for anyone who hasn't been broken before. only they know how it feels to love a lonely existence and come out of it smelling of victory. a closeness is arriving. a jubilant calling will be with you soon, sweet child.

<u>*Numbness*</u>

i feel myself beginning to pull away even further from this world and all the facades and shoved images it puts in front of my face to wash this brain of every truth i believe in. there isn't much that is sacred anymore. there isn't a touch that feels real, not even from my own hands. to find meaning, one must lose what they love the most. to find love, one must break their own heart to know how it feels to be betrayed by someone who is there for them. i know nothing if it isn't you whom i seek out between the light and secret. my needs and desires are too simple for this place. i could sit and do nothing but write, drink my coffee, and call it a lifetime well spent on thriving in the midst of decaying. time is measured in the places we feel most alive. death is measured in the moments we cannot find a breath. i was born to observe from a distance, from a closeness only a few can survive at being. for us who choose to be sober, we are attacked daily, but nothing will repel me, from me, not even you putting my heart through your stake. i once loved you in full. now, you are a full-on shadow of what love looks like when spreading its legs for a fool.

<u>H.O.P.E</u>

it's all agony until someone tells you
how your struggles kept them from ending
it all. you never know when opening up
becomes an invitation for another to
feel safe to do the same.

<u>*Safety In Scars*</u>

love will remain in the cracks, spaces,
and in the faces of those who will take
your memory further away from who i
am now. your scar is safe on my heart.
it is all i have left to remember that you
did love me this one time in your own
kind of forever and only.

<u>*Permanence*</u>

nothing is permanent except permanence itself, and even then, every breath is flawed, every thought inescapable. you can try and starve yourself all you want, but the hunger for more ultimately destroys us in the end. it is how we find our line and when and where to cross it if needed.

<u>*Believe Them The First Time*</u>

i spent years proving to you i was good enough. towards the end, before you left, i learned you will never give enough to those who walk through life without knowing the difference between enough and over-used. my tread has worn down again, yet, i am running to a place somewhere beyond humans and the faces they use to get you to believe every word they tell you is true.

Erasing The Path

you'd think i would get tired of writing about her. the one who broke me over a full moon i fell in love with. the one who showed me what it was like staying up and learning that love is a language not everyone speaks. your voice was my favorite sound i ever felt. it was how i knew the difference between night and day, between safe and running away. there will be a piece of you in every step i step. there will be some days, when i will retreat a bit to feel you again, then cover up the footprints to forget how it felt to be loved by you. to forget how to get back to you all over again.

Everywhere Beyond Here & Now

these days seem to go by longer than once before. do not be afraid or timid of what is to come. you were born with a wildness only given to those who know how to wear both a halo and set of horns. you are not meant to be made out to be who others may have thought you were. fire and glory define you, as do the constellations you inspired to shine on long after the shine is gone. there is no one like you and your power remains full at all times. scars and wounds do not define you. some of us carry our own art with us at all times. being here now after everything you have been through will forever be how angels sustain their flight and fight. you are love in every season. you are love and beyond what it means to us who have never felt it, but know it is out there, because you showed us by giving your time to bleed for it.

The Remedy and Reason

someday, you will forget about me completely. i am not sure if it's a relief for me or a silence i will carry willingly. every time i turn out the lights, i imagine you waiting in bed for me, all smiles and comfort laid peacefully before me. i needed you more than any heart needed a body. i can feel your eyes on me, just like the time we sat across the room from one another eating pizza and wondering what sitting at the same table would feel like, wondering what the other tasted like in anticipation. you are a wound turned to scar, turned into some nightly ritual i write about that no one reads. i wish i was braver than my singular fear of telling you to leave me. i am in awe of the hold you have on me when you are not even mine to hold onto. you're in bed now, probably reading with socks and a hoodie. regardless of season, you are always cold. it's still precious the way i see you. we all want someone to make us feel less alone. i honestly do not know what broken is like for those of us who were born with it inside of them. i do my best to keep it together while fading further away from who we once were, of who you were for that part of me that felt broken all the time.

<u>*Golden Hope*</u>

do not just take my hand. take my body to where you are. lead me, never leave me. i am not a lost soul anymore. i am yours, holding, waiting, loving. there is nothing more i can do with my life if it isn't finding a way to you, in the life we are in and the life that will find us next when this one calls us home. we are the devils and angels of a past life, yet, you are the hope i still believe in.

For The Dreamers

when i think of you, i think of the sun
painting flowers on you and laying down
with nothing but love to show for all of
the days i spent alone. how lucky are the
dreamers of this world, to spend half a
day here and the other half alive and wide
awake loving what we do not have now.

If You Think You Can

she asked me if i still believe in love, in giving all you have left to a feeling you cannot describe, but can feel when you wake up to a warm body beside you. i told her about the time when the moon drifted down to save me. she went on to ask me if i was scared of ever getting hurt again. i paused slightly in astonishment, surprised by her ability to know when someone carries a pain caused by someone who said they would never do it to you. i told her, no, because i believed that someone, and you cannot hurt those who had their heart ripped out while you watched it keep on beating for a life that died the day they left with it. there is still some good left in me, and that is what i am offering to anyone brave enough to try.

Sundresses & Bare Feet

many won't believe me when i tell them who you are. sundresses and bare feet, with enough love to hold an entire world upon your shoulders. a beauty resides in you that reflects hope for those who were raised to be broken. tattoos and the ocean are your therapy. you are a constant worry for the evil around us all. it is why when everything seems to fall down, you remain steady and the tallest in the room, knowing the end is nothing more than knowing who you are when everyone else is running away from it. i know you have been through your own hell, which is how i can tell your eyes carry a golden love for open roads and full moons. i may never be able to hold you, but i know you are in good hands with a universe that loves you.

Right Time. Right Person

i have felt the hands of love before.
before these scars of mine settled into them.
i was once just a broken display of human
remains until you collected me into your
arms and traded away my pain for the
love you had been saving for the right time.
i do not know if i am the man you had
dreamt about when you decided on who you
had hoped to find later on in life, but you are
who i saw when i closed my eyes to make my
own wish all those years ago now as a child of
war and tireless poverty.

<u>*A Love I'll Never Know*</u>

bringing the devil to his knees has been your greatest strength and victory. it has been a love all on its own not many ever have or ever will have the guts for. you are the most remarkable woman i will never get to love. in some ways, it makes knowing you all the more bittersweet, but i know humans cross our paths sometimes to stay as long as the lesson needs to be taught and for however long the feeling needs to be written out.

<u>*A Sun's Surrender*</u>

be still, breathe in the warm air of a sun's surrender. be still, live amongst the shine and adoration from all things producing a feeling to feel intently. these days will give way to beauty again soon. remain full at heart and unbounded, in magic and serenity.

A Spark's Reminder

for the books we never think we will have to write. to the love we never think we will have to live without. there are remnants of past lives scattered across the waves in our madness. shout from the depths of your soul and bring it all back to life. may the spark inside never be forgotten or unloved. may it never be put out or let go of once it has felt the epitome of what it could be.

<u>*When Spring Arrives*</u>

there may come a time when our lungs are not be able to breathe in the vastness of this lifetime, but the expansion is as sweet as our surrender is. we must have faith in something that takes us beyond this spirit we call home. before we were given a home enclosed by this rotting flesh, we were limitless, we were something humans could never live without. be your own musing and rise once again through fire and light. the whole world is waiting for your spring to arrive.

<u>*Where New Life Is Found*</u>

the heart desires everything it touches, everything that touches it. and when it cannot have it, it will eat itself whole. i once told you that you were dead to me, but you're still alive in my dreams. your skin still a honey glaze with a river running through your soul, full of gold i could never sift through enough. i need new landscape to walk amongst. a place where deer and wolves are abundant without worrying about the other. i need to walk through more shadows and light to fully express myself truthfully. i cannot keep coming back to the dead for inspiration. i have used every bit of flesh and bone to write the last twenty books or so. i need new life, a place just for me and my unrequited use of love in my poetry. i need reserved peace on a river's bank to watch a shimmery light-show of constant flow from madness to restful sleep. i am growing too old to not be in love with where i am at. i do not want to age with hate and regret being the only lovers that know me well.

Maybe It Was All A Nightmare

it was over dinner in Sedona, a nightly shifting romance in December, when i looked at you and told you, you spoke like someone i could love forever. maybe it was a fevered dream from a tethered rendezvous of souls meeting before bodies were given a proper calling of inhabiting precious things. your eyes never blinked once while telling me about your darkest days in college, a childhood without innocence, and how you felt defeated and lost before you found me staring back at you in a way you have never had anyone do before. i would have stood with an ovation for the way you carried my heart away with a gradualness reserved for the dead. i gave you flowers today. the ones you said you wouldn't keep because they reminded you of how everything dies. i walked by your shop today and smiled as i saw them in a vase you bought at a thrift store two blocks from the place where we ate. i do not know if love is a real thing anymore or if it is something we are programmed to say when someone sees us and doesn't turn away, but i have your eyes, and you have mine. maybe one day our bond will be forged in the stars.

<u>*Where Will You Take Us*</u>

if i were to give you my hand, would you walk, run, or go back to bed? i've waited on you since the first taste of summer flashed upon our skin. there's been a dullness to life, to living, ever since i began to beg for something sweeter than your lips. i quit tasting them around the same time i found your name coming out of my mouth instead of the sand i had been eating. lover of mine, you may have been. stranger of mine, maybe you are now. when i ask the moon for a love to never leave me, i hope it is you who shows up with naked shine and an open road for us to get lost on. i do not know how many more days i can hang myself out to dry before the devil mistakes what is left of me for someone he can take. one day, i want to roll over in bed and see your eyes closed full of dreams. i want to take my right hand and place it softly beneath your spine. roll away with me, sweet infinity, roll away. you have my heart and i will play the part of the fool if it gets me closer to the edge of everything we do.

Gentle Squeezing

some days your voice is quiet, a mumbled retreat of love and all of its reasons to embrace, instead of leave. i do not know if i am forgetting you, missing you, or realizing you were never here to begin with. i have held flowers so tightly, i killed them and their meaning. i never loved with haste when it came to you. you deserved to be held and kissed slowly, a dying wind's approach to breathing when being or doing anything more would have been the death of it. your beauty is in the touch, in the seeing, in every way a human becomes a living work of art by not pretending it is something it's not. i have seen mountains fall to their knees when you are near. i kissed you once and knew i would never kiss anything ever again. i was an unmarked grave until you gave me purpose and reason to spit out the same earth that had chewed me up in the first place. i lay my head between your legs to feel innocence and a sense of comfort i was not born with. i feel them squeeze around my neck hard enough to know you need me, to know you could not die without me. in this life and the next, it is your heart i will always feel in my chest.

Love Of Fire And Flames

i could remember you as you were, but you were mine back then, and now everything you helped me with has burned down around me. i am now playing in the ashes, trying to find you again beneath the embers. being raised in the flames, you believe at an early age the rest world is a raging bonfire, too. you grow up reeking of smoke. you wonder why you are the only one with burnt fingertips and red eyes. we both knew what we were getting into and what kind of life it could have been if we had been able to water each other rather than adding more fuel to what was taking shape within our life. you tasted like war, just as i did. anything we involved ourselves in got buried in the back where our secrets went. every time i see an open flame, i think of you. these cold nights make missing you hurt even more, but i cannot go back inside to save who i was and warm myself for the sake of being happy again where happiness was a ploy we both used against one another.

A Remember When

i had a dream last night i was out with Zach Bryan, his girlfriend, and a few friends. the good never die, but the good always put up a glorious fight. slamming guitars and taking out the stars. when there is a love, there is a body who has been without good enough. may our scars guide us and remind us of what is possible, of what it feels like to endure and have what is ours to outlast these struggles bonded to these mercurial bones.

<u>Love's Stitches</u>

there are days i feel better. i feel as if the world inside of me has come back to heal again, to kneel again, to surrender in love. then i see you and crack into fault lines and fall apart at the stitches each star has beautifully given to me after you.

<u>Do Not Pass Along</u>

do not give someone else the pain of what they taught you to feel. you will only end up killing two spirits and a lifetime. two souls that deserve something better than a lesson never to be remembered.

Every Phase Of Her

one can never forget the moon once
you know where her light comes from.
once you know the woman who wears
her smile. once you know the side she
never shows is just as lovely as what we see
during our lonely nights.

<u>*For Protection, Not Persecution*</u>

love lives on long after the sword is pulled. long after the wound heals. long after the last one who said they would defend you, but left their mark on you in a way you never saw coming. there is no choice when it comes to love. it is decided long before we know our own name. it all comes down to surviving who you think is there to protect you.

<u>The Bird Still Singing</u>

my hand may always know yours, but love ends for all dreamers once they are awoken by the lie. truthfulness has always been the one thing we kept sacred, but when secrets no longer hold the soul, we must go our separate ways. we must become a bird without a view from above and not below the tree it fell out of.

<u>*Witness*</u>

whomever comes after this, whomever thinks they can manipulate you and bully you into being someone you are not, they will have a fight as grand as the moon to go up against. you will make it, i have seen it. i saw it today.

Empath

there are times when i feel nothing at all. other times i feel every goodbye ever said, whispered, and thought of. i am not a human with an empath ability. i am an empath with a human disorder to feel, and feel intensely every permanent emotion meant for me or not. i am fighting not to be different, but to be whole.

Every Hour On The Hour

i have memorized your laugh, smile,
and soul. i know your flaws, demons,
and sleep schedule. i can always tell when
you are up. it is when i feel you the most.
it is when i know you the best. when 2am
calls on you, i will be right beside you
when 3am calls next.

Saved Chances

there is not time here in my life. there are moments of regret, moments of remembering, pauses when i am sure good things still happen. there is a single day of feeling which leads me to the next act of becoming. i drink my coffee and think we are all our dreams coming into the light the first time. we are all alive, running away from our deaths, from the fading facades we hide behind. some days, you will never find me. most days, i can barely find myself. but i am here, underneath every version of who i have needed to be. a broken heart is still a home, just as a broken man is still the wanderer i am. counting my the moments on my fingers, i know there are still a few saved chances left.

Cannibalism

the only thing left to do is love you better, through the hurt and broken parts you believe yourself to be a part of. my heart has no room left for anything that isn't you. sadness visited me today along with the outline of your face. when i reached for it, it left me just as the rest of your body once did. maybe one day the space i feel between heaven and hell won't be so one-sided. i cannot wait for anything that told me it won't be back. but here i am, stuck in-between holding on and letting go of a name that comforted all of my belongings not belonging to me. you lifted me up just as the light of a brand new day gives everything it touches enough faith to trust in an upheaval of loss and pain. i did all i could to keep you. sometimes, it is better off losing what is irreplaceable. it teaches you how a human can be consumed by its own heart and still have enough left over to try and love again.

<u>Home, Sweet Home</u>

sometimes i wonder if i will have more than
i do now. if i will ever make it back to Utah.
i miss the life i had there. i miss the struggle.
i miss the freedom of being on my own.
i miss so much these days that i have no clue
how much it is actually missing from me.

<u>*When Logic Is Divorced*</u>

i wish there was a way to be closer to you
while i was away. i wish there was more of
me to give, but maxing out my love for more
than what i have now has been tiring and
counterintuitive to where i need to be,
versus where you want to be.

<u>*All Of Her Secrets Safe*</u>

looking at you, knowing all the bad i have done, i finally did something good with this life of mine. i probably never deserved the moon to shine her light on me, but i will never stop finding ways to keep her secrets safe throughout my day.

<u>*Elemental*</u>

most nights i miss traveling and staying in
hotels. i miss standing underneath the
shower for an hour and allowing the scolding
hot water burn me the only way it can.
muscles relaxed. mind cleared. i am free
for the only hour of the day where nothing
is thought about and not a goddamn
thing is felt besides the water,
the moment, and silence.

<u>*Ageless*</u>

there is still life to be found beyond these bones of mine. i hope it is you there to greet me when i finally find myself. i hope we can make it across this great divide that has divided us for the last decade. i am growing older, as you are, and i know the only time is now for what we want to accomplish together. i hope you never forget what i told you when i said, i'd still love you at ninety the same way i loved you when i was thirty.

<u>White Padded Room</u>

i wish there was a better way to get you back, an easier love to deploy. i wish you wanted me as much as i do you. i wish this wasn't me writing about you still. some lovers never leave. they just kill you in the process, in the inability to move on when you know it is what you should do if you are to ever gain another heart that loves the insanity out of yours.

<u>Conservation of Light</u>

i am after more than the stars show me in my darkness. i am only lost when i am away from you, away form the soul we share. if there were to be a me without you, take my name and face away from me. i do not belong to this place if it is not you by my side. if it is not you looking back into my eyes. i will walk this life in shadow if i must in order to conserve my light just so you know all i have is yours, only.

<u>A Magician Never Reveals How</u>

my entire life has revolved around missing someone or something, giving too much or not giving a fuck about something entirely. i have never been keen to a balance of any kind. i have had vows prepared once for a woman i loved dearly and a broken soul to show for it. i have allowed the absent feelings from others to dictate how i feel about myself. there have been moments of bliss tied to these heartstrings in hopes of it being flown above the pain and agony associated with who i am. i have felt unworthy because of my desires and emotions going unmatched. some days i wish i was born to not feel everything at once and fall as easily as i do when someone takes time to listen to my cries and silence. this year will be a turnaround year for me. a year of giving less to those who show up one day then leave the next or leave my messages on read. i am too old for anything less than what i give to myself. a philosophy i am investing more into. i know what is meant to find me, will. i have outgrown the lonely within and by those who tell me they want love, when all they want is someone to make them forget their own.

A Rose No Man Can Hold

you are floral, all bouquet and colorful. what you do and how you do it is from another time. an era of smiles and jubilees. there will never be another who look like you with a nakedness only flowers can show during a vulnerable season of change, during a wilting of shyness and benevolence. your violence is violet, all caught at midnight between half and crescent. a deluge of moonish behavior, you ascended mountains before light could touch basins and all the shadows attempting to bring you in. your movements are priceless, a direction without cardinals and degrees. a smile so subtle, you would miss it if you were hoping for laughter instead. the day misses you, but the night knows you better. it is where you find comfort when running tires you from within.

All Fire Or Nothing at All

my life will never be for a kind of love that does not lose its mind when it comes to kissing wherever and holding whenever it is needed. if your love is lacking effort and affection. stay the hell away form me. my age is not how i feel, but it does tell me if you are not bringing fire to the table with me to burn everything we have ever been told is what love should be if behaving means sacrificing who we are for who we need to be.

The Joker

what could have been will always lay next to me as the empty space replacing what no one or any one thing ever could replicate. there is you, then there is everything trying to be. you are the hero my life needed for the villain i had become in mine.

A Broken Forest

you are a splintered forest within me. each time i feel something new, they dig into me even more. every time i see beauty or what i perceive to be from another world, they dig and push further into this body. each time i believe i have new love to give to someone who makes it all hurt less, i find it to be deathly. i need another part of nature to walk through, to sit amongst the dead and newly born energy one finds while decaying and healing with everything else doing the same thing. my branches will be born again. i will find new light to love me, starting from within.

<u>BLUE</u>

maybe i need someone as sad as me, as lonely as snow during summer's awakening. a heart like this can only be understood by someone who knows darkness as old as my childhood. some of us cannot be reached by regular eyes and hands, humans from the other side where light finds you every day. some days i do not know myself well enough to love what i see, but i try. i trace the face with shaky fingertips and timid acknowledgments of knowing, of almost being able to nod my head, yes, at the questions it all presents. i am at my best when reflecting fire and frowns, writing what others cannot see or describe. i walk just fast enough to keep the shadows where they are, behind me and choking on the past they are made of. meet me where i stand and i will take your hand and meet you at your lowest. i rise before the sun to know i am alive before anything else knows it is not. meet me where blue becomes a smile we both can share and carry to replace what we could not rid on our own.

Where We Are

we are all after something, a constant chase of a new sun, a new moon, somewhere beyond the place we are currently at. i could write for days, fight for years, but i am choosing to open each day with love for you. in order for us to be true to ourselves, we must begin where our heart awakens, where this incredulous life restarts each thought and ounce of hope we have left to offer to it and to anyone looking for change.

<u>Widely, Sweetly</u>

it has been years of constant overthinking, never realizing how easy the simplicity of living really is. i do not feel it often, but belonging to someone like you makes the years already lived before finding you mean more. the losses almost overcome me. this is life for me now. your smile, being alive with you. what a sweetly smile it is to bare.

<u>*Say It Now*</u>

together, flowing in and out of where we want to be. a calm force you are, a brilliant cast of harmonious sensations you will always be. i will never be who i once was. a million excuses without purpose. i am not here to fill your life with more emptiness than you already tell me you have. my mind remains restless, but my heart is full of promise for you. unbroken and made strong by the gods, there is a vow somewhere in my throat trying to reach you before it becomes something else i should have said sooner.

Sound & Color

taking your hand and feeling you next to me has been a love i have always wondered existed. some days, i do not even realize the infinite, but you show me how limitless being here can be. love has many names and faces, but none of them have ever had your voice. it is my favorite sound of sunshine. it is my favorite color of life itself.

<u>*A Morning In December*</u>

laying here wake at 5am, unable to rest properly. coffee is the main source of getting my mind right. i hate waking you up. i probably won't ever be that person. in the same breath, i need my alone time, too. i need my space from the world before the world knows i am up. i am currently on my second cup of coffee now. it is below freezing outside. the heat stirs through the rooms, suffocating at times, but needed. love is here, and love knows my intentions. you are still asleep, all blankets and comforter, you keep me warm right where you are.

<u>*Beyond Functioning*</u>

chicken, veggies, then coffee to smooth out the corners of the day. it has been the most beautiful afternoon here. we walked a few trails. took the dog out for a walk, and now making dinner. i only have coffee past a certain time once i am out wandering. i believe all things become more suitable and acceptable once you break your routine. never become a moving body without intent and purpose beyond waking up and going to bed.

Where Life Is

i do not really know who i am until i am in an unfamiliar city. scattered across sidewalks and walkways where strangers before me have came and went. where they have fallen in and out of love, and could never get back or have returned what they thought would be forever. it is the most surreal feeling. to be amongst the lost, the pursuit of artists must constantly roam and create new roads for others to use for themselves down the line. the branches of life, we are and become once our roots begin to develop a certain unquenchable thirst. once they realize they are a part of a grander landscape.

<u>*Exponential Costs*</u>

between the spaces of a sacredness,
there will be a time and place for the
beauty you seek. it is all around us,
always guiding us to another version
needed in order to notice the value
of everything. life has the most
expensive price tag, but if you want it
to be cheapened, continue believing the
bare minimum will get you by if
extraordinary is what you are after.
if living is what you lacking.

<u>The Hyphen</u>

these words have been given to me like an orchestrated secret i keep hidden until i need to express the moment. there will always be clarity by the way you feel, live, and love. the deepest connection to oneself is dug out over years of self-awakening. we are never a finished product. our rawness becomes our imprint, our dash on concrete above our sleeping bodies.

Checkmate

i have always wanted to find love, but not because of me selfishly imposing myself onto a feeling i was creating. maybe naturally, organically, it would feel better, but even then, i believe it will play out the way it needs to, regardless of what we do. fate is the checkmate of life. to be in the moment means becoming an entire lifetime being played out before your eyes. there is so much to learn about anything that moves us. the only true thing we can do is sit with it until it becomes a part of us, as we move through life together with it being a reason why we are better and more complete.

The Climb

some people are attracted to one another beyond the intimacy this life gives out as what constitutes as being normal or sufficient. the connection becomes an entanglement of desire. what becomes the meaning of life itself will remain the question all seekers seek out. maybe love isn't what we are after. maybe it is just us trying to make all of this matter more than what it ultimately gives us back in return for the sacrifice, for the climb.

<u>*Why Do You Sleep With*</u>
<u>*Your Head Underneath Covers*</u>

at least i got to love you as i did, for as long as i did. i know it wasn't for nothing. later on in life, i will still wonder about you as i do now and see you all smiles and closed eyes right before we turn the lights out. if comfort ever found me, it was underneath covers hiding my face next to your shoulder.

Beauty Defined

i never wanted you to carry my burdens for
me nor did i want you to love these scars
i thought were hidden so well. you spoke
to me like a dream, like rings of smoke
leaving a gypsy's mouth. i came to you before
you knew who i was, but you had already
held me once before when this body
barely had bones and this mouth had a
tongue. i am decorated in darkness, a lovely
texture of callus and stone. i thought
i needed to be someone else for you to
love me, but you stood next to who i already
was. love is not a secret i keep with the
moon anymore. it is all in the way you
move, as if beauty never knew what
beautiful could do when being witnessed
by someone who could finally see you.

Walking, Talking, Laughing

i wish there was a brighter eye in my life. one with a cherry shine and golden skin. i take my breaths deeper now, keeping out what doesn't belong to me. i have been raised by sin since i was old enough to know my wrongs were never going to allow my rights to win. i have caught up to my past and passed it along to the me that died in order to keep this version alive. i do not know where a heart goes when it breaks. i only know how vacant a body feels during its decay. one day, i hope to understand it all better than i do now. i hope i still see your face and sweeping smile when i get lost in a crowd. the bricks my mother used to shut and mortar my mouth are finally chipping away form years of rage and lashing out. my kindness comes in waves and nearly drowned my very existence, but you kept my lungs afloat. you gave my body a soul and my fears the peace they never surrendered to me until you chose to stay, until everything was still and quiet inside. my words have their limbs back.

<u>*Sacred & Safe*</u>

take me back to the start of it, to the beginning of it all before we got lost in the shuffle of a loaded deck. take my hands and tell me you will keep this heart above the sea, above the enemy in me. love nearly killed me before i turned twenty-five, and now i sit with you, telling you how you loved this exquisite violence from my mind. give me breath and i will give you the moon. give me hope and i will return you back to the beginning of everything good, everything shining, gleaming and freshly formed. you have given me a new found glory, a separation from the hell you pulled me from. hold me and i will hold you, until life becomes infinite and hallowed.

<u>*Orphans & Acceptance*</u>

i remember days of never belonging, a feeling of not being a part of my own life. there will never be a day when i feel normal. some of us are meant to remain outside of a body that may never feel like a home we can rest in. there are movements i make that i am not sure belong to me, with thoughts i know have no place being mine to begin with. i do what i can with them, turning it all into poetry for a chance to have a place within its life to love me one day for taking care of them for as long as i did without giving up on them, as those who told me the same thought they would be able to.

<u>Angels And Their Gifts</u>

i was probably more capable back when i had this head of mine secured on these shoulders, instead of in a moment of weakness trying to love before i was able. only birds and angels know how to fly, which is why i cannot believe what i see when these eyes of mine catch you hovering above me as you smile down at me. then just as i blink, you're off again to show others how a lovely human is the miracle of all miracles.

A Nightly Stroll

i do not know who lied to you, but you
cannot chase down the sun. i have tried.
between the drugs and white lines on mirrors
and roads, there is no hope to try and
capture what does not want to be a captive
of any kind. i gave up the feat but defeat
could not keep me from chasing down an
encounter from you; all sunshine and moon,
all gowns and lamps looking for rest.

<u>A Moonly Teaching</u>

there are a million ways to live and only one way to love if you are open and willing to accept it. we must trust ourselves when the time calls for us to become more of who we need to be. take your scars, wounds, and bruises as far as you can in this life. we are not what they did to us, but we are what they have taught us. be gentle with yourself. not everything will make sense as it happens, because at the time they occur, our lives are not ready to accept its pain and teachings. be soft in pursuit of all things wild and precious. we are only as infinite as the moon is when it comes to light and love.

The Dance We Take

there may never be another moment than this one when stars collide and this earth we are rotating on feels like home. there are moments in this life that feel like days and others that feel like decades. i can only hope you find the minutes that take you where you need to go and where your life becomes more of an endless sensation of grounded gratitude. breathe in the cosmos, sweet child. allow your lungs an intently, sweetly personified perfume of vastness and a parting glance as the sun falls beneath your eyes. your power has always been a courageous act of mild violence consumed by beauty, an effortless appeal to the soul you are, to the love you seek, and the life within you dancing freely within your naked spirit.

Eternal Hope

i never wanted to become who i turned out
to be, but i always had the strength to change.
even if rock bottom tasted like defeat and
sour whiskey, there was hope for me.
i turned all of my scars into birds with a
song to sing. i know who you are hoping to
become one day is possible, because i have
seen hurricanes become a sanctuary for
the lost and displaced, for the damaged and
the damned. i have seen miracles look like
humans giving what was left in their wallets
to someone who was without pants and shirt.
you are the fire others tried to use against
you. you are the heaven we all hope to go to
after our season of lonely is finished making
us and turning us into ghosts of another life.

<u>Mourning Light</u>

i've thought about you incessantly today. with my head in my hands, nearly consuming my own identity as a man. there are things i wish i could tell you now, and again after they have been said. maybe you are better off without me. maybe you will never need anything i feel for you. if i was given a few minutes of your day, i would say, you are not mine, but i still hold you as if you are. once you attach yourself to a certain beauty, everything else feels like death covered up the sun when they decide to leave.

<u>*An Unorthodox Counselor*</u>

you have endured more than your fair share of loss, of heartache, of unknown struggles you never openly speak about. i know your shoulders slump over before you lay your head down. living is not for everyone, just as loving becomes another word said to forget we carry it all home when it left us where we found it. maybe remembering you doesn't help me, but at least it shows me i am capable of doing more with less, with things that no longer serve me purpose other than creating new poetry to write about for someone to use as a guide to get through their own grief.

Architect

i love you too much and that is why it will never work. you are there and i am here, both figuring out what it is we need and do not need for our own paths. i wish beauty was easier to keep, like a rose without thorns, like a smile without a hidden pain behind it. i know i didn't deserve all of these scars and broken thoughts, but i have done my best to make the art i thought was best for me because of them. i have always tried to do what was best for me when it came to writing, living, loving, and leaving. when you protect everything at an early age, you forget how to allow someone else to take over and help you with it. you forget you do not have to suffer alone. you forget you do not have to go at it all on your own. you forget that staying silent is only as good as the company you keep. i bit off my tongue years ago. i tore out my insides the same day. i am so fucking tired of hurting which leads me to hurting others who do not deserve it, when all they want to do is show me what i try and tell others about love. my resistance to it all has given me nothing but more walls. i am ready for the beautiful laugh to find me once and for all.

<u>*Speech Therapy*</u>

there has not been a day when i have not tried to better myself or the situation i am in. some days it feels like progress and other days it feels like i am walking backwards with my hands tied and eyes sewn shut. it is hard to make out if i am doing anything right other than healing what i feel will never be done. i wake up and it all hurts the same. i wander through my mind long enough to hopefully tire myself out by the time night asks me if my tiredness has raised the white flag or if it is still folded tightly underneath the memories i cannot escape. i have been tongue-tied since the days of being in speech therapy, trying to help me with R's and S's. my mind has always worked faster than my mouth. there is no such thing as being worn out for me. i pretend to rest just so that i may fake out my body enough to sleep. i do not have a difficult life by any means, but there are countless days when i wish i was not this person with all of these voices telling me what i have done can never be forgiven, released, or unseen.

Hopefully Hoping

i hope one day you find someone who is able to reciprocate what you always give unconditionally. i hope you never have empty hands or a heart longing to be heard and felt through someone else's chest. i hope you find someone who knows what it means when your body shakes without warning, not because it is weak, but because they know how to touch you. i hope their eyes remain on yours when nights make you both blind to what you need. i hope tenderness is never lost or forgotten. i hope your mornings begin with a kiss that could keep you alive until a new one was created. i hope when you feel yourself going into hiding, you have someone who will find you, who will run to you in a fullness that will put all of your fears behind you for good. i hope you never know what true missing feels like, and if you do, may it be corrected before you believe what others have told you, showed you, and made you believe.

Unbridled

i hope you are beloved beyond the human you are, beyond the mess you think of yourself to be at times. i hope you dance and embrace the rain with someone who won't make you drown in it. you must remember that those who drown in the shallows were only taught by those who couldn't swim in the the depths where you were born and raised. i want love to scorch your fucking heart with an unbridled sense of worth and meaning. i hope for everything beautiful to find you so you never forget what your face looks like when you feel your hands begin covering up what was carved and etched by the gods themselves as a reminder to what beauty is and where it was found to begin with. i hope you get the beginning you need and the happy-ever-after you desire.

<u>Spiritual Outlaw</u>

there's a place you go. your own church with trees and fresh air as your stained glass windows. a cathedral just for you. a black top road with just enough white lines to guide you. you fall in love even more with life itself by simply passing by everything you put to the side and opening your eyes to new beauty around you. a sight for all to see, to take in, to know what living actually means. there is a place for your kind, out beyond the hills and away from your mind. maybe heaven is that for us wanderers. a piece of existence where going too far is never satisfying. where staying within the built-up walls and confines we often construct to keep out those trying to destroy what took an entire lifetime to find. your broken is someone else's beautiful, someone else's end to all the suffering it took to finally find someone who gives a fuck about you. that is my religion. that is my mother mary and the fruit i will eat until i finish or until life is finished with me.

<u>Somewhere In The Middle</u>

you were in my life last year. you were on my mind every night until i knew you were gone for good. i keep solid and fluid memories of you stored safely in the pockets of my heart, reaching for one here and there to get me through the day. my words will remain full and all yours until they, too, run their way out of my life. i have borrowed more than time could ever give back. i do not know if i will ever be able to. not without you with me. not until i have you back here to make my body feel again. to make my hands and legs work again as they once did when i knew how to be human by watching you live and breathe. sadness came to me today. it sat beside me, wanting and needing to show me healing will be on its way. they know each other as lovers of a another time and place, just as you and i do. i believe it will find me. i believe we all go through certain stages of misery, of unbearable grief to know ourselves better, to know who we are and who we are not. some days, i am miserable, too much so to even give myself a chance at anything. then there are days like today when being in the middle feels good enough to love my honesty and the absence you gifted me.

<u>*Reincarnated*</u>

there was never a more secret place than between your arms and legs. a beloved rapture captured so precise and lovely. a touch of hands can go a long way when years have gone by without human interaction being nothing more than passing a stranger on the other side of the street. we stripped our fears of their power that night. we did not have to beg the light to hold us together. we were there, as one, inventing new ways to come undone, to lay still with a million movements being done by our souls, our eyes. all it took were a few minutes of pausing to correct our alignment. you turned a boy into the man he never knew he could be, because of a past he could not let go and shake free from. you were a blessing from the gods, a reincarnated belief of being stronger than i was. you handed me life in the palm of your hands, and i gave you back everything i had saved from wandering around crowded rooms meant for those who felt safe. dancing and laughing in front of others. it was you who brought out pieces of me i had accidentally cut others showing. you healed the monster and animal i always saw myself to be, the one who almost ate himself to save others from the hunger pains.

Three Of Life

i could tell you a million words, but i would only need three. on my back, hands and knees, or upright walking, striding with an nakedness only given to those who are beside themselves, full of intent and flame. three words for a lifetime. three words for the right time. three words for the moon in you and sun in me. three seconds to leap into and out of your chest. three minutes to kiss the flowers on your breasts. three hours to lay silently in-between Jupiter and Mars before coming back down to earth where you are. three days for the eyes to see it has always been you and how it will never be for someone else. three months for the light to touch the scars not talked about. three years for the hands to hold firm between a sea and its storm. if anyone has ever known you, it was me. if anyone has ever known you for the things you never talked about, it was me. three words for a woman i would write a million more for. in haiku, soliloquy, in prose, in sonnet, in poem, in ballad, in life and in death, i love you.

Continuum

we all have choices and decisions to make
that will change our day and lives. when i sit
here, in front of this machine, in front of all
of my mistakes and setbacks, i learn more
about who i am and why i am alone at this
point in my life. nothing has ever come easy
with me being who i have had to become to
not only survive, but write in a way that gives
me clarity and a newly repurposed mindset
to carry with me all the way to the end.
humans have several names for life, for love,
for loss, for a memory. some of us look for
things we will never find or have to pass
the time to in order to forget about all of the
humdrum we are going through. my life is
lived by and through the poetry i write,
through the goodbyes and good nights i will
never say again. to everything living that has
closed its eyes for the final time, each one
knew life to be a certain way, a rhyming
convulsion of words and heart beats born
from poetry. i am looking for anything
that can make me smile again, to feel again,
to laugh as if i wasn't born to feel this way
forever. i remain in continuant search of her.

Widowed Feelings

i still walk around with my shoulders weighed down by guilt and shame, a burden buried between my shoulder blades and the middle of my spine. the taste of my youth and teenage years remain inside my cheeks and underneath my tongue. i have done my best to wash out what i could not smoke, drink, and suffocate out. i was given Thor's hammer and a set of bloodied brass knuckles as a kid. i found myself fighting anyone and anything to make up for the child i would never get to be. holes in the walls and doors were a language it seemed only i could speak or write about candidly. i gave everything i had to a mother who could not love me back equally. it laid the foundation for the rest of my life. it stained my heart black and my soul red by the time i thought love had at last chose me first for a change. the emotions i could not let go of, turned into ungoverned and unattended anxiety and depression. i have been happily pleasant and present a few times in my life. the kind you sit with and know its arm is around you, never tempting the other side of you to come back. happiness is my widow.

<u>A Precious Hate</u>

last night wasn't the first time you told me you hated me or at least parts of you did. i remember the time i hated you after what you did. i know none of what happened is anyone's fault. i will never blame you for hating me. i thought i was ready to go all in after showing my cards and darkest parts to you as you did with me. i think hate has always been something i have heard since i was a boy after hearing my mother yell and scream at us in a drunken rage about how much she hated us. maybe that is why i do not get easily offended anymore when someone says it to me. i know there is plenty of blame to go around these days for a lot of what is happening, and you feeling that way about me does not make me love you any less. there is love somewhere within that word when you use it on me. i would rather you take it all out on me now while you feel it, instead of down the road when i do not see it coming, along with you leaving. thank you for your blunt honesty, your precious ability to communicate what others shove back down their tightened throats to choke on later, which would kill any chance they would have at happiness appearing.

Hunchback of Notre Dame

it feels like i have broken my back on the knee of everyone who told me they would never hurt me. walking more backwards these days, with a hunch all of Notre Dame could use to make fun of each deformed part about a darkness they know nothing remotely close to ever being. the open road airs out my laundry, my twisted and wet thoughts about life and the sanity we ultimately lose in search for a reason, for a cause. i am sitting at a piano typing this. if only i could play the ivory as well as i whistle the blues, life would make more sense for the nagging dubiety within me. take your autonomous aim and shoot while you can, while your hand is free from shake and second mentation. love will repeatedly cost you at least one life for the two it tells you it will give. my heart is bruised with the color of your name.

Persephone

you have this beauty about you, a way of leaving the entire room feeling loved and understood. it was more than a glance you shared. in barely a moment, you shared your entirety, your whole life with a paused breath before eye contact was made. if Persephone had love to give, she would give you in its place. i see your hands go behind your back, crossed and hoping, with fingers made from leaves and twine. you speak about a life you once lived, a place where you were creating the world you wanted to grow old in. you have not aged since then, all golden hues and leaning against the sky. your tiny frame could still be home to a million moons, all calling out to you as if you were their mother. i have seen you stand a day back on its feet, positioned precise and perfectly to ensure a comeback for you both. i have loved you here and there, but mostly in my dreams. maybe i will have a new day soon. one full of unobstructed views of your laughter.

<u>*The Removal*</u>

never allow what you know is temporary to ever become a routine. it is a dark place where the light knocks and you continually open yourself up to it, expecting there to be a human standing in front of it. it is one of the implicit and quickest ways to have your entire life rearranged where your heart is in your throat and your mind never believing in love again. i wish peace to fold your corners and smooth out all of the glass shards still lodged in the areas where love was supposed to be there for you while you were away from your own body to allow it lead you from the pain.

Sandcastle

we are not our pain. we are not who left. we are not our graves. we are not what we have been without. we are what matters when it means staying. you are the love you give to yourself. to be someone who has gone their entire life without ever believing a single thing once told and spoken out loud, means knowing one day it will all change for the better once you open yourself up to the proposition. listen intently and freely to the truth within listen attentively to what the silence means when you are rounding out of your life and shaping it into what you need from it. there is no replacing an emptiness someone gave to you, but you can rebuild where they left you with every single piece.

If Only I Had Listened

i remember telling you when we first started this, that i would go one day at a time with us. somewhere along the way, i got lost and caught up in the future. there is nothing wrong with thinking ahead, but when you allow it to overtake your rational thinking process, giving it power to control all of the things that won't happen instead of focusing on what you have right now, you lose sight of what truly matters. and what truly matters right now is, us. because right now is my favorite day of the week, month, and year. it is my favorite, because we are together and we have each other at this exact moment in time. i tell myself often, "do not take this for granted. do not take her for granted. not everyone has a right now. some only have yesterday to love."

When Wolves Become Homesick

i will continue to feed the wolves while you are away. they have grown into loving beasts since you left. they watch the moon with me because she reminds us of you. the howling is becoming louder the further we get into each month and the brighter she gets. i do my best to keep them busy and away from the fires they consistently desire to run openly to. i know they get it all from you. they are such a loving force, a promising touch of a reality and truce where you find your way back here some day. i know you are doing all you can to hurry, but please, sweet light, take your time with it. we will be here. this love, inherently full of embrace and patience, will be here to greet your return. the wolves looked at me today with the color of your eyes. it was a remarkable transition of who they love the most out of us. but i, too, side with them on all aspects when it comes to you and your fixity.

<u>Outside Of A Pine Box</u>

maybe it was all bullshit, some delayed gratification meant to be called love when it really wasn't. we got hung up and tripped over a million ways to say, i love you, without ever fucking saying the words. feelings must match actions and emotions must attach to expressions when nothing else makes sense. this rattle of twisted death and tapping of bottles on a treasure chest must be some form of music played for this heart of mine that is mute and deaf. you see, i have screamed as loud as i fucking could at it when i was younger, wanting it to move and strike what my tiny fists could not. i wanted it to show me how to write, how to shine, how to love what could never be mine. "i do not belong here," i scream out now, in nature, in harmony, in hellish elements made for the bonely skeleton i have become. the tongue of mine i have chopped off to save my words for whatever world comes next. maybe then it will make more sense to speak to someone who knows what nothing means. maybe then a pine-box will smell of life and breed new hope for the dead it fills its dirty mouth full of.

No More Shoveling

i go to bed with a heavy and broken heart. it's not until i see the sun that i realize i have survived another night without you. maybe there is a commitment within this wretched day of finally letting you go without any more reminders of you. may this day be all i need in order to throw away the shovel and plant what is left of you in my mind into the ground. i can only hope tomorrow there will be nothing left of you in my life, in my eyes, in anything you have touched of mine. learning how to be okay since you left has been the toughest challenge for me, but i am doing it. i am making it.

<u>*Wave After Wave*</u>

lean into me with a belief i will believe in. summer is getting closer. i can tell how your sweat falls a bit faster before you get into the shower. i am not sure there is anything i love more than to be near you in some capacity. knowing you are closer gives my life an abundance of paths to take and chances i will find you again should our souls meet outside the flesh. the sun shines today with a slight, but meaningful breeze out of the southeast. the infinite humidity crushes dreams down here, but i am all in, betting on summer to return you back to me, just like ocean waves returning home from war.

<u>*This Is The Way*</u>

yearly mementos of life and death. each tear a victory of a wounded warrior. each bruise a true love story. each breath called a different name. each minute detailed by hours and days that were not fully lived. do not dare waste these battles you fight and have fought. there is no such thing as not showing up when that is the only thing this journey asks of you. if you do not, it will show you what happens to those who turn their backs on it.

When Lies Become Fruitful

when you leave, because i know at some point you will, they always do, all i ask is for you to leave me better than when you found me. even if it is another mark and reminder on my skin, another flower planted within the flesh, awaiting someone else to bring their light and water. leave me for good, for something you can love entirely. not just for the feelings and words i have told you that you were never fucking brave enough to say back to me.

<u>No Vacancy</u>

i told myself years ago that i would not give myself to someone until i was able to take my own hand and not pull back. it has been years living with a hesitancy for a residency, as a roommate, as a reason for being this way. i only wish to know your face better and how you learned to smile as openly as you do. i want you to be my last breath, a loving gasp of collected thoughts and adoration for being a butterfly to me when all i had known before you were dead things and plastic wings without love to give reciprocally.

<u>A Full Lifetime</u>

may this be the one for us. the remarkable moment, the noble touch, the solidified embrace, the substantive kiss, the morning of rolling over and knowing why you never want to leave this bed, your side, your eyes, your lightly love, your perfect shape that fits and holds us both together, with your legs squeezing us and keeping us as one for an entire day, a full lifetime.

<u>*Hinges*</u>

when we meet someone after years of
wondering if we would ever find a human
who felt and aches as we do and have, it all
becomes clear. we both become the hinges
that keeps each other together and allows
one another to walk through, hand in hand,
gracefully, wholly, and accepted.

When Lonely Leaves

there's a type of lonely in her eyes that make mine feel understood. i have never had such a feeling come over me as to someone finally seeing me for the first time. it felt as if the sun and moon had seen each other before the cosmos knew what to do with them, as if my soul had been welcomed into this world as fresh as dew on a grassy dawn. a turning point, a new-sprung beginning, a forged belief that i would never go another day being forgotten by someone who never wanted to be without me. i gave my breath to her, and in return, she gave me these reverberating words to write the rest of my life all for her, and her alone. my speech is nothing but her soul coming back home to rest.

The Light Never Broken

and then it all comes back together. it all comes back to you, and you believe again in something greater than loss. having nothing and thinking you have something are the same thing, but it only takes an extra interval, one percent more effort to pull yourself back up again. wipe off the blood, and get back in the fight. we are the light never broken.

Firestarter

ravens may never be quoted, but your name will be sung throughout time. beating hearts cannot die without being heard one last time. chaos is nothing more than insanity catching fire and combusting with truth. and when it comes to both, you are the flame, the torch, and all things red and orange compressing the cosmos together in the way only you can.

<u>Giver, Giving</u>

and that is how healing works. you believe it and you stop feeling as if you have to tell everyone about it. your silence is the same love the sun gives the flower. you do not have to tell everyone you are okay. you do not have to give or unleash proof as to why you are better today than they thought you were yesterday. your bruises will heal, just as the heart that has been overtaken by grief seemingly does before grace is shown.

<u>Assistance</u>

there is so much to be thankful for, and my happiness and belief in it feels good again. my past is healing along with my heart. this hard fought smile finally fits onto my face without any force needed. it is there gracefully and with a full sense of pride and purpose. the help of others is all we can hope for when it comes to assisting who we are and the journey we are on. it was something i thought i would never feel the realization of anything being real again.

Plant As You Grow

you will dance alone until you are ready to take the walk back home. you will dance down the hallways as if you are in love again with life and yourself. you will come to value all things, past and present, as if they were always supposed to happen exactly as they did. growing up means planting new seeds everywhere you go, knowing you may never see what comes from it.

Dreamers Versus Sheep

you have been on your own for so long now, everything seems more complicated when being around others. solitude is not a punishment, but rather a way to know we are good enough for ourselves. bravery is a simple rebellion not many have the stomach for. it is how we differentiate ourselves between the dreamers and the sheep.

Even If It Shakes

i hope you find someone who knows how to love you when you do not have the strength to do it yourself. i hope you find someone who never sees it as another burden for them to carry. all it takes is one time, then they will know you can give it back to them whenever they are in need of it, too. some of us require a little more help putting ourselves back together in the morning before the day begins. if you do not ask for it and rather suffer in silence, your screams will never mature into vocalized words others need to hear when it comes time to aid you.

<u>*Breaking Bad*</u>

she's the giggle during the most quiet of moments. the stare you cannot look away from. she will destroy you, but only if you hurt her first. she is everything you think she isn't. being who she is has cost her a thousand lives, but if you insist on making her out to be the villain, you will become one who knows how it feels to be pushed beyond their limits as she forces you beyond the cliffs where only you will go to die.

Simple and Assured

love consists of light and a touch of darkness. there is not a perfect balance, but some humans merely need one good day to know another one is on its way. all it takes for some of us to know we are okay, is an arm around our shoulder blades and a single word to know being alone is something we do not have to be anymore.

<u>*A Spark Of Light*</u>

you speak of love, yet you are finding it to be tiresome to embrace your own body. you are as mighty as any strike of lightning. you must believe sparking your soul against the most tender part of your heart and seeing just how much fire you are made of, to see just how spectacular it is to create a feeling by simply teaching yourself how the earth speaks your name softly, but always maintaining self-worth in the form of acceptance for everything you are and everything they do not know you to be.

<u>Orbital Existence</u>

some days, i forget everything just long enough to remember my own happiness still exists. each day, i get closer to its permanence. each day, there is more truth to be found and less ache for me to worry about. i am learning how to be an amended man, soul, human, and something more than just someone trying to exist within the orbit of a life not many will ever find themselves a part of.

<u>*Steadfast Struggle*</u>

there will be days when you feel everything, when you cannot escape your own thoughts. but it will pass. the struggles we face are only meant to strengthen us, not collapse us. they are only here to teach us what we can live with and without. not every day is a promise, but the steadfast struggle, the one that seems to take all of our energy when we need more, is a truce and guarantee configured by life and death itself.

Enimagtic

i would have loved you beyond the very breath, beyond the touch, beyond the goodbye after the sun and moon left us both. you were not supposed to leave, but all beautiful things do. all things that can speak and say the word, love, emphatically return to where they belong, with us or without us.

Forged By Forever

i hope when you see yourself, you see all the victories you have fought to keep and hold. i hope your heart is healed, beating, and wrestling with the sun, moon, stars, and all the cosmic things. your story is far from over. your story is how the rest of us know that we made it, too.

Nonexistent Hesitancy

you do not know how much violence it took to be this loving, to be able to turn it all around and live again. my tears may say one thing, my smile may often say another, but both will annihilate you if you perceive them as my weaknesses. i have lived too long to allow and give power to something as simple minded as your absurd and out of touch misunderstanding to summarize who i am. i haven't been forced to cross a line in a while, but i will not hesitate when it comes to my peace of mind and yours.

Roll Over To Roll Away

and now that you have found someone else, i hope i can do the same and give all that is left to me that you did not want. i know it wasn't my fault how things ended the way they did, but a part of me will always wonder what life would have been like if you had allowed me to love you more than what you said you needed. i will always wonder what coming home to you would have felt like and sitting down at the table to eat what you had made for us. i was lucky enough to know how it was to lay with you, and that is how i still feel you. when i lay this body of mine down and roll over, i remember vividly how you rolled over on top of me for the first time to allow me to see how much you did at one point in time want everything i was to you.

Ethereal

not everyone knows how to be around her, and i find that to be a beautiful characteristic to have. there is this innocent way she throws the sun around to where she needs it on any given day, at any given time. i have never seen anyone be able to take a ball of light and fire, and place it anywhere except where it wanted to be. to say she is human would be a lie. she is the furthest thing from it, and if anything said to her would be taken as a compliment, i would hope it could be something as marvelous as that. every Sunday, the sun appears to be closer to me than any other day, which is why it is still my favorite day, which is how i know she remains close, even in shadows and gold.

<u>*Beauty Remembers*</u>

be brave amongst giants. sweet child. you are
one of them. you have always been one of
them. wherever you go, the light follows.
wherever love goes, the beauty remembers.
it will wait an entire lifetime for you.
it knows what you have been through.
it knows you, oh so well, sweet breathly.

<u>*Unconditionally*</u>

there are many humans we will meet in our lives. sometimes, all it takes is one to change your life, heart, and path. if you know her, she will never give up on you. she will do whatever it takes to make sure you know how much you matter. you will never forget her or her desire to love without needing to be loved in return.

<u>*Wings Of Glory*</u>

that is when she is at her best. that is when victory becomes a true living thing. there is a certain hope in the broken, in the frayed, in the edges of an existence beyond this parallel of breathing. you must move with conviction, with an abundance of purpose to remain uncaged from those who want nothing more than to capture the purity of everything you are and all the things you make them feel.

Through The Trees

they come back. they always will. they always think they can. they believe you stayed who you were when they knew you. some make it back. others stay out of your way. a select few are hell-bent on destroying your peace and what you have built without them. fuck them. live your life anyway. though a single tree removed from a forest does not necessarily kill the group, it does bring a different light because of it. we grow as the company we keep. we are not artificial. our feelings and actions fucking matter. good or bad intentions, they all have a dear cost. i sincerely hope you are where you can see yourself and not behind someone who will never share the universe with you.

Survival

she grew up with dreams being the only thing worth keeping. nights were her escape, lending out ways to seek out magic. she never allowed anyone to be close. it was her way of protecting everything she loved and would love. it was her way of making sure she could survive what had killed her innocence growing up where the only things nurtured were chaos and its mother.

An Overly Existence

maybe you gave up too much to those who were okay with losing you. you held onto broken things, because it kept you from believing you were, too. you never understood the concept of over-watering, over-loving. being overly made and living in a place that simply wants to take it all away by returning you back to normal.

To Calm The Rattle

there will always be a fire we must walk through. we will be tested relentlessly until our breath can finally move the trees. may your wild never know defeat. may your tender bones only break for the meaningful, for the enlightened aspects of your beliefs and wishes. may they heal all the same, in a wholly togetherness, profoundly kissed by a lovely truth and purpose, raging on like mad men finding a religion to calm their rattle.

Worth The Squeeze

they tell me life doesn't begin until you are forty. i laugh at those who say such things, because for me, it all started before i was born into this barren land. i have roses for eyes and driftwood for hands. out here in the hill country, age means nothing. it all begins with how your soul feels in the breeze brought on and filtered through pine needles and limestone. you do not get to live until you have died a few times, and i, well, i am only thirteen in afterlife years. we do the best we can with the life we were born into. you do not get to choose anything besides the road you are on. make it last, toast and cheers all you can. the last drink is always worth a squeeze from the fruit of the fallen, from the rebels, from anything make-believe.

<u>A Trick For The Mind</u>

it wasn't timing that ruined us. it was never being able to be truthful about what we wanted. in the end, you waited for someone who wasn't me, and i kept on loving you all the same. i still wake up and think you are here, then the sun goes down, the moon comes up, and here i am, still in a place where you are not. each time i hear the door open, i will never not think it is you finally coming back to me. i know my sanity was lost at an early age, but my madness is what makes me believe in the magic others will never fucking see.

Life Of Lies

you kept me inside of your hands like a wish you never spoke out loud. we were friends who walked together up and down our own lives where no one knew who we were. it was more than a love we shared. it was a secret we would always keep between ourselves. it was a hidden meeting place in a parking lot during mid-day to eat our lunch, hold each other, and talk about a future we ended up never having. it always ended up the same, me getting back into my truck, looking at you, then you turning left and me turning right, not knowing if i would ever see you again. those days fucking haunt me in my sleep, knowing i could have kissed and loved on you more. but the truth is, your body wasn't for me, just as your soul wasn't mine to keep. you belonged to him long before you found me. i just wish you could have told me the truth, as i cried and screamed it out of me for you to know me and my demons better.

Final Swing

when it comes to you, i do not know how not to be all out. you have been something more to me than any other kind of feeling i was born with. the type that life would try and kill, but only poetry could save. so here you are, resting your breath and body in every line i write, making sure you have enough love to make it outlast whatever is out to get to you. you belong to the night, sweet light. your eyes always knew the way to the other side. they always saw what others could only describe in passing. i know you better than the gods who gave you life and lightning. for you will remain the final swing from the mighty sword you carry and raise.

<u>*One Step At A Time Treatment Plan*</u>

i may never get to approach you again. the way a sunset walks towards you. the way a sunrise slows your heart. the way birds carry more than an unbridled sense of empowerment when morning makes their wings become a living thing. i may never venture close to your energy ever again. it is a deep and wretched sadness felt through my bodily form, felt through the earth's shivering core, felt through every scar on the moon's face. it was you, and i will never not believe it wasn't you this entire time that gave me reason in something greater than this one step at a time treatment plan i am now living and hoping to find love in again.

Comfortably Comfort

there will be days when everything you feel now will lead you to a greater place of acceptance for who you are trying to become. we may never fully be aware of our power. i hope when the lights go out, you never go far in-between dreaming. I hope you never go a single day without being told how much you are worth and how meaningful your embrace is. there is comfort in all things, but in you, it is ad infinitum.

A Beautiful Truth From A Beautiful Lie

do not look to me to save you. i have done it before, or i should say, tried. they took me down with them. beneath the oceans, above the sky, down below the belly of every whale that survived captain Ahab. i could never breathe on my own. i could never see without crossing and tripping over my vertigo. saving someone who only needs you when they forget who they are, is the knife slipped between your ribs slowly. it is the marking of evil you will never remove, and you will go your entire life believing it was all your fault for every bad thing that happened to you. there is hope though in all of our brokenness. it is ultimately coming to terms everyone is out for their own reasons and none of them will impact you unless you give it power to. i am still learning how to cut the cord they gave to me as a gift and said it would keep me alive. all lies are beautiful, until you know why they were said to begin with.

Once. Twice. Thrice

when the love is done, cover me up with the moon and carry me home. we may never get this chance again, so bend with the wind and lean into me until i have your full heart in these heavy, but generous hands. if i were to ever lose you, i would lose the sky itself. my undefined and shapeless life would become tasteless, colorless, and uneventful for the crowded spaces within me needing all of my senses to comfort the wounded i carry deep inside of these humanly created pockets, empty and laid down in curses and cursive i was taught to use as a young kid still growing into his trapped and cluttered mind, which blatantly assisted and enabled my stuttering speech to stay with me for thrice the time it took me to lose it.

<u>*Sweeter. Stronger. Numb*</u>

i am nothing more than the absence of you. my voice and howling broke the sky years ago. maybe i am in need of forgiveness or maybe forgiveness already found me. some days, i am too unsure of it all, which leads me down every path I ever took alone to find more of me, to find more reasons to choke on words and feelings handed to me as if they were candy i was a naive kid looking for something sweeter, stronger, anything to make death not taste so familiar.

<u>When It All Tastes Like You'll Be Okay</u>

if i am to ever find my way again, i know for the sake of safety and survival, these broken parts of me will need to hide for a bit longer. darkness is not only a friend of mine, it is one of the last parts of me no one has ruined. it is one of the last things that has yet to break me more than a human has, even though my own darkness has been the closest to dying i have ever come, there is still some sort of comfort it brings, just as you once did when you were looking at me in the eyes, speaking and spilling lies that i savored and digested as some sort of truth for the homeless waging wars inside of me who were tired and restless without anywhere else to go, but you knew how to fill their tiny bellies full of what you knew would keep the starvation from killing them.

Homes Of Ash

some days, i don't know where to put my grief. i have filled a thousand caskets with my dead, put all the flowers into the fire, called out each feeling by name. i still hope to see you again. in a world that doesn't separate love from breath. i never did belong to anything until i met you. you corrected my posture and taught me how to speak without speaking down to myself. once you have lived in a burning house, you never think anyone will have the bravery to get you out. but you did. you still do. i still smell of smoke and your sweet breath trying to calm me and bring me your air to save what was left of me.

<u>Choking On Air</u>

for those who leave, it may only come in waves or a few ripples at a time. but for the ones who are left behind by them, drowning seems to be the only way to remember them. and every time you come up for air, you choke on it, because you forgot how to function. you forgot how to be good enough for yourself again. you forgot how to be good enough to even take in a fucking breath you know will save you. you forgot it all, because you allowed it all to become them.

<u>*Listen Intently To Me*</u>

when you do not hear from me, please do not take it as me not caring. i have cared too much for too long. i have loved you just the same. when it comes to you, i will be here with a thousand ways and an endless energy to smooth out what stirs inside of you and makes you believe thoughts of you being alone and forgotten. i wish you didn't believe your thoughts as often as you do. i can lonely hope to help you with that if you will give me space and room for it. if i am good at anything, it is being able to overdo and outdo whatever you think you should be given.

When Goodbye Became You

and when i catch you looking over at me as you sometimes do, i'd swear you love me right then, but i know you do not anymore. maybe it's not that you don't, but rather you cannot at this moment. and that is why i will continue loving you, even if it isn't reciprocated. i hold out hope for the one day you will again, for the one day this hurting returns my easy breathing back to me. and if you never come back, at least i knew how it felt to fall for a moon who always remained and rose for me when i didn't need anything more than another voice to drown out the one in my mind. i still hear you every full moon when the sky is yellow and kissed with black covers with tiny reasons embedded within it to know it will all be okay some day for me, and all those who suffer as i do from all the life, love, and horrors that sneak up on us. when goodbye became you, i knew where to go to find my solace. it is the one gift you gave to me i cannot let go of.

www.ingramcontent.com/pod-product-compliance
Lightning Source LLC
Chambersburg PA
CBHW012022110726
47994CB00012B/3270